Dedicated to:
Nick, Erin & Family

Written By: Abigail Gartland

Hello, my name is St. Dominic!

I was born in 1170, in Spain.

One of my uncles was a priest. Even when I was young, I saw how special the priesthood was. My uncle taught me so that I could become a priest too.

I was a very hardworking student in school.

In 1191, a famine spead across Spain.

There was not enough food for people to eat.

I was so sad to see people hungry. I sold everything I owned to buy food for the poor.

I spent my whole life helping people. I traveled around the world to share Jesus with others.

One day while I was praying, our mother Mary, appeared to me.

She handed me a string with beads on it and called it a rosary.

Mary told me to teach people how to pray the rosary. She said that praying the rosary will bring people closer to God.

I founded a religious order called the Dominicans.

After a long life of sharing Jesus with others, I went to Heaven in 1221.

Do you want to be more like me?

You can celebrate my feast day on August 8th.

I am the patron saint of the Dominican Republic and astronomy.

pray for you every day of your life.

St. Dominic, Pray for Us

Copyright:

Clipart: © PentoolPixie © LimeandKiwiDesigns
Licensed purchased: 1/10/2024

About the Author

Abigail Gartland

I love the saints and I love my faith. The idea for sharing the stories of the saints with little ones came when my dear friends were expecting their first baby. I wanted to create something as unique and special as our friendship. Each book is dedicated to very special people and groups who have enriched my faith in different ways. I am blessed to write these stories and appreciate the unending support of my family and friends. When I am not writing, I am a middle school teacher. I hope you enjoy these stories. I pray for each and every person who opens one of my books to learn more about the saints.

Abbie

www.ingramcontent.com/pod-product-compliance
Lightning Source LLC
LaVergne TN
LVHW061632070526
838199LV00071B/6658